DEAD GIRLS POEMS

BY FRANCESCA LIA BLOCK

FABULA RASA 07
A MIDSUMMER NIGHT'S PRESS
New York

Poems © 2019 Francesca Lia Block.
All rights reserved.

Cover art © Elisa Lazo de Valdez *www.visioluxus.com*

A Midsummer Night's Press
3 Norden Drive
Glen Head, NY 11545
amidsummernightspress@gmail.com
www.amidsummernightspress.com

Designed by Nieves Guerra.

First edition.

ISBN: 978-1-938334-24-5

CONTENTS

DEAD GIRL SONG 7

PART I: TALES

THE WITCH 11
THE WOODSMAN 12
THE DEMON WOLF 13
THUMBELINA 15
ASHES 16
CHANGELING 17
ROSE WHITE, ROSE RED 19
HANDLESS 21
DEER BROTHER 23
SKIN 25
BLUEBEARD 27
TWELVE DANCING PRINCESSES 29
THE LOCKED GARDEN 30
THE BLIND PRINCE 32
BABA YAGA 34
ICE QUEEN 36

PART II: MYTHS

PERSEPHONE AND DEMETER 41
PSYCHE 42
ORPHEUS 44
EURYDICE 47
HARPIES 48

CIRCE AND ULYSSES 50
PSYCHE AND PAN 51
TO HADES 52

PART III: FABLES

THE SANDMAN 55
DEATH 56
PROGENY OF EVILS 57
TAM LIN 58
THE DEVIL 59
FREAK SHOW 60

ABOUT THE AUTHOR 63

DEAD GIRL SONG

We're very popular these days
Why wouldn't we be?
smiling in the photos before we were taken
young, pretty and missing
But there's another reason
(We'll tell you, later)

The ancient Greeks liked us, too
made us flowers or trees
And those brothers Grimm
brought us back with a kiss
(It's not always so simple)

Think of the transparent coffin, the wall of briars
Think of the lake filled with flowers
where our hair floats like roots
These may sound pretty
but we're so alone
We suffered more
than you'll ever know
And if you kiss us
we'll still taste like glass
(And soon we'll start to rot)

But you'll keep worshipping our memory
We hold a mystery you sense but haven't solved
In us She is carried down through time
(In us She lives)

PART I: TALES

THE WITCH

She's there all the time with her poison apple heart
She can't help the fact that she's growing old
while the young girl blooms more every day
snow skin showing blue river veins, and camellia pink lips
But the witch, she could stop
raking girls' scalps
with arsenic combs

There will always be Snow
There will always be mothers
pleading with mirrors

Heed my advice:
Take your heart from your chest
Let it bleed in your hands
Talk to it softly
as if to a lover
or a white stag
or to a mirror
Do not take a bite
or use it to choke her
Sing to it gently
then put it back
into the empty
cavity
of your chest

THE WOODSMAN

He takes up the length of her bed end to end
His skin dark, then darker, against whitened sheets
scented with sap, amber and smoke

She wants him here
where she can touch
and forever suck
consume, be consumed
in this bower of heliotrope, larkspur and rue

But she knows she must always let go
so he can report back to the Queen
with beast's blood on his hands

The Girl doesn't mind though
not anymore
She's learned after that one year stint in the forest—
chop wood, carry water, fight monsters
who covet your eyes
and your soul—
that it's worth it to have him come when he can
saving her life with each thrust
while she saves his

Look at her callouses, her sinew and scars
She's Woodsman, too

THE DEMON WOLF

Like the wolf in the story
it grew inside Grandmother
a tiny fanged thing, furred
making her bleed
Then it grew larger
The woodsman tried cutting it out
but it left him wailing, with his head in his hands

He staggered off crying, "Demons!
Finally it grew so big it ate her
I got down on my knees and asked it to eat me too

She was small as a child lying inside of it
The foul smell made us choke
our skin and hair slick
with blood and entrails
I waited for the woodsman to come rescue us
but he was long gone
staggering to his mother's bed

Grandmother turned to me and whispered
"Darling, you do not belong here"
Her eyes flashed in the belly gloom
Go now"

I took my axe called Poetry
and cut my way out
The demon wolf dissolved around her
but she was gone
I bathed her body and kissed her cheek and dressed her in
                                                          fresh linens

I buried her in the garden
where the red roses grow
and no demons are allowed, no more

THUMBELINA

i've had to be small
bathe-in-a-seashell size
sleep-in-a-matchbox size
hide-in-a-teacup size
so that i'd be love-able
i've had to stop eating
to fit into his jeans
to fit into his arms
to fit on the futon
to not consume him
no new york times list
no hollywood movie
no red-soled shoes
no meat, no dairy
no days without exercise
no feeling too pretty
so as not to outgrow him
so as not to lose him

ASHES

She did the tasks every day—
the cleaning of ash from the hearth
the sweeping of leaves in the parlor
the clearing of vines from the walls
the sorting of shells that the sea had swept in
the freeing of moths from the bedroom

Slowly the house began to turn
to its former state
a pale gray villa carved with roses
pink marble floors
pale blue ceilings starred with crystals
murals of cherubs and clouds
bed fit for a prince
wardrobe of shoes made of glass

All of this, it does not save her
eventually everything
still becomes ash

CHANGELING

I was forced to live in the hotel lobby
the carpet was scratchy, red and gold
wood-paneled walls and the smell of booze and smoke
No place for a baby!

(I think I remember something else
shallow water rushing
over stones? Green daisies floating and a hillock
with a door? The smell of rain cupped in petals
music like the wind
playing her silver hair
someone I loved
someone who loved
me?)

But in that lobby
without rain or wind or any
thing you could call music
one lady fought revulsion
and took pity on me
big and pale with my bobble head
swollen, half-blind eyes
and an old man's voice

She carried me upstairs
laid me on the bedspread and dressed me
Then she fed me from a bottle
though I made her queasy

She knew she had to learn compassion
I'm that part of her she hates

ugly, weak, abandoned
severed from my illumined world
not loveable apparently

But someone has to do it

ROSE WHITE, ROSE RED

I was Rose White twice
both times Rose Red was raven
much more beautiful than I

Rose 1 painted lilies
emerging from the dark like candles
We ate sushi in the shapes of flowers
She studied medicine, got all A's
Her smooth eyelids
her runner's thighs
her slightly feral grin
I was so young and scared
There was nothing to fear
She might have saved me
if I'd let her

Rose 2 was a musician
We giggled on her dollhouse bed
way up the canyon
wearing only bras
danced to 80's songs
in that small dark club
as if no one else were there
attended neon raves
galleries filled with art we didn't understand
We were always sweating
trying to cool the back
of hair-strewn necks
in the night air

I should have kissed Rose Red both times
Instead I lost myself
to the devouring
Bear

HANDLESS

Sacrifice:
I was sold to the devil for gold [1].
I gave up my hands for my father [2].
I gave up his wealth to go wander [3].
I gave up my freedom
for one gold skinned pear [4].
I gave up my child for a changeling [5].
I gave up my life for my child [6].

Reclamation:
I gave up my kingdom for forests [7].

Redemption:
I gave up my king for an angel [8].
I gave up my hands made of silver [9].
for hands made of flesh, made of bone

1. The devil had braided haunches stuck with burrs, steely hooves, a tail like a bramble and horns bursting forth from his forehead as if they hurt him. He saw me by my father's apple tree, pink and white as apple blossoms, and wanted to take a bite.
2. The devil would have killed my father when he would not give me up so I offered my hands instead. The devil cut them off at the wrist with a cleaver. My own tears stopped the bleeding, and the stumps healed up like doorknobs.
3. My father became rich and offered me a room in his big house and a servant to clean and feed me, forever, like a child. But instead I set off into the world with a sack on my back and my two polished stumps.

4. In a gated garden I saw a pear tree. On it hung a pear the color of spun gold. My mouth watered—I had not eaten in a day. I stood on tiptoe to reach it with my mouth. The king saw me and took me in. He was rich and handsome with large appendages. He forged me hands of silver because a king cannot marry a girl with missing parts. I became his wife.
5. The devil stole my child and put in his place an elf-locked fae.
6. In order to save the changeling I had to leave in exile, never to return.
7. With my child I came into the forest rich with sap and mulch and the dark trickle of secret waters among the roots. Here we found an abandoned cottage made of willow branches and here we lived.
8. The angel who found us here is tall as a tree and his hands are like wings. His skin is dark of hue. His smile a pearl necklace. He has no money in his pockets. He has no pockets. He brought me pears and water. He helped me feed my child.

   He loves my strange-eyed boy, changeling or not.
9. The angel wept upon my silver hands
   and they became
   hands of flesh and bone

DEER BROTHER

I told you not to drink from the first spring
and you did not become a tiger
I told you not to drink from the second spring
and you did not become a wolf
You would not listen when I told you not to drink from the third spring
and you became a deer
Your eyes are still brown, lined with long lashes
your fur the same burnished shade
Your hooves and tail never make me forget
that we once shared a womb

We live in the thatched cottage deep in the woods
I wreathe you in columbine and primrose
We eat nuts and berries
drink our fill from the stream by our door
No witch has poisoned it with the spell of beasts
You no longer speak
but in the evenings rest your head upon my knee
and gambol in the redwood trees by day
briefly forgetting your grief

I worry for your safety when you roam
but cannot control you any more
than when you dipped your face to that third spring
the silver water tainted, witched but oh-so-sweet
redolent of mint

I know hunters roam these woods with guns
and bleeding bucks
Once I saw a witch
her face depraved as Stepmother's

and I wonder if she came with the reminder
that she had cursed that spring
and took you from me

But no matter the danger
Some day we will venture forth from these woods, dear brother
We cannot live alone forever
I grow thirsty for a young man's love
as you for that water
Now I understand

For human hands upon my throat
I would risk becoming animal, become a ghost

SKIN

Before my mother died
she told my father he must only marry
one as fair as she
one who knew domestic arts
and could please him in the bedroom as she had
So on my twelfth birthday
when I brought him cake made with rosemary and wild
berries and my tears
not knowing what she'd told him
he looked into my eyes and stroked my skin
presented me her ruby ring
for he had taken it
before he buried her
and I could almost see the phantom of her finger
pointing from within

I looked at him with Mother's eyes
and told him only
if he found the magic deer
that roams the woods
would I be his

He sent out his men to find her and they brought her back to me
She reminded me of Mother
and I wept into her fur
begging her to save me

Thus I was transformed into a doe like she
and I ran fast and far
with the king's men at my hooves
until I reached another land

There the prince he captured me
in his golden net
and brought me to his castle
where I was fed and watered
free to roam as I saw fit
the secret woods

We shall see if he
loves me enough
to let me remain a deer until I'm done
or else I'll be a monster
half-human and half-beast
chained by the throat
my father's daughter

BLUEBEARD

Bluebeard had enticing eyes
dark as danger-lakes
He was graceful on his skateboard and had a throaty laugh
He said
"I never noticed you
until the day you wore those high-heeled boots
and then I thought, hmmm maybe her?"

He took me to his chamber
and wooed me with sweet wine from fountains
and with dance and music
The lyrics went, "tear you apart"
but I chose to take this figuratively
the speak of pop, not literal

He shot my portrait
smiling at him dumbly
like an animal unaware of slaughter
He brought me swooning flowers
took me to dine in canyons
strung with fairy lights
and where coyotes howled

I let Bluebeard do to me
whate'er he wanted
I let him into places
no one else had been
I wrote him poems everyday for months
and he responded
with emoticons

When Bluebeard sent me home
alone in the dark
when he danced with another while I watched
when he refused to acknowledge me in public
even with a glance or smile
I should have known
should have been grateful
instead I stuck around
one day too long

What scares me about Bluebeard
isn't that he killed me
but that I let him

TWELVE DANCING PRINCESSES

How did they find each other?
across a map of light
that connected souls
words they recognized
sending out the signals
feral
petal
blood
bone
smoke
luminous
lucid
bruise, burn
marl
until they danced forth from their secret rooms
across electric continents
to the wicked witch's ball

They stayed all night until feet bled
they were locked up
and bodies fed
with tubes

The only thing that saved them
were the words they scrawled
revealing all

For freedom can't be kept
from a girl (or twelve, or more)
with pen and wall

THE LOCKED GARDEN

I ate the bitter plant with the same lust I felt for being with child
gulping down handfuls of shredded leaves
the only thing I'd stomach
before nausea hit again
My mouth and eyes watered
Rapacious, I climbed the fence
tearing my silken petticoats
I got down on my knees in the dirt
scraping my chin with twigs
my knees embedded with pebbles
I would have eaten the moist earth too, but the king, my
                                       husband, stopped me
He took me in his arms and brought me home, but each night
                                       I escaped, went back
sucked on the plant, devouring

When my child was born with her long green hair
scented of leaves
and her sepal eyes
the witch who owned that garden threatened me with death
if I did not give my daughter up
I refused
ready to die in an instant
rather than lose her
I'm a mother after all
I wondered how I could have ever loved a plant when I held my baby
with her tendril fingers

But again the king intervened and at twelve
she was gone
taken to the tower

a young woman with breasts as full as mine and long colt legs
skin like roses white, torn from witches' gardens
her hair a stair of green but not for me

Everyone talks about her fate
and the fate of he who saved her
but I'm the one who suffered
the true loss
Me with my great hunger
I'm the one who made
the gravest
mistake

THE BLIND PRINCE

When I fell onto the thorns
they tore my eyes

And so I stumbled darkly
lost without you
green-haired maiden

My sockets, they are empty
caterpillars nest there
and the seeds of roses

How could I have ever
taken sight for granted?
Angry at injustices
I saw all around me
the beggars in the street
the dying children
gunmen
global warming
my own weakness
my secret fear of you

Now I wish to see it all
to help, to grow, be worthy
to overcome my terror

But I can only stumble
feet gnarled like roots
beard thick as moss
tendril fingers reaching
for you maiden
in my sleep

Believing I smell violets
I wake with dried leaves only
crumbled in my hands

A heart as dead
as both my eyes

Maiden, if you live
someday perhaps you'll find me
This time your tears will heal me
give me sight

Eyes will grow, fresh in my head
like two small animals

BABA YAGA

Listen, it's not like you think
Those girls? They came to me
They wanted things
gold and jewels and love and everlasting
beauty
They wanted my white steed of morning
my red steed of day
and my black steed of night
my prophetic cat
my loving dog
and my singing bird
They wanted my house on its claws
because it could walk
They wanted my servants
tied me down to reveal
their invisible forms
and secret names

The girls beat me, bruised me
called me crone
They made me listen to them weep
about how lonely and ugly they felt
(they with their long skeins of hair and poreless skin of glass)
as if my withered face and spotted hands
my empty bed
were irrelevant

Yes, I killed them
and used their skulls for lamp posts
with candles lit inside
brighter than minds

Yes I took their lives
But you can see my scars

If you come visit me, pretty one
I'll show you the truth

ICE QUEEN

"I'm so cold," my mother said
"Come warm me
There's a lady in the room"
When I arrived
at the small Spanish-style apartment
with white roses in the front
my mother was all jutting bones
in her little pink pajamas
I tried to thaw her
I didn't see the Ice Queen
but I knew she was there
watching us
taloned fingers long as hands
skin a silver blue
and her touch a burn
punishment
like I used to feel
sticking my tongue into the ice tray as a child

I didn't beg my mother to stay
My brother and I sat beside her as the day turned gold then gray
then black
through the shut windows
"I love you" we said, again and again
all we had left
all there was that mattered

It did not melt the Queen
her gray eyes were pools of frost
black lake of something

waiting underneath
It did not make her leave
but when my mother
smiled and took her hand
someone else arrived
in that dim and musty room
someone my mother recognized
someone she'd been waiting
a quarter century to join
someone who had once been
fire

PART II: MYTHS

PERSEPHONE AND DEMETER

Trapped underground
skin tattoo-blue
a closet full of missing shoes
and pairs that crushed my bones
destroyed my feet
dust and crumpled silks and sweaters
an empty page
a blank canvas
a pond clogged with dead weeds and the bones of fish
yellowing grass
a dripping faucet
the sound of her voice no longer in my ears
no music at all
no dancing in the living room
no dancing
food without taste
her, gone
ashes unscattered
still in their urn
we're still afraid to touch them

Grief is the underworld
Persephone's realm
a single pomegranate seed
life without Demeter
Did anyone think
that the daughter might have grieved too
even with Hades to fill her?
And mine comes so briefly
Mother, mother
"Under the ground"
she would say
"is where the seeds begin"

PSYCHE

I think of arrowheads of obsidian found in the earth, polished and rough hewn able to kill or simply to rub between thumb and forefinger as a reminder

I think of gods with wings rustling on the windowsill
In the still of night
Never look at them in bright
light
Never speak too much when they are here
Be silent, reverential

I think of longing limitless
that frightened off too many men
Or caused me to send them away
thorns tracing blood from skin
cracked music and condoms unused

Psyche's sisters told her he was monstrous
And then she burned him with her fear
I refuse this
And it's not why I light the sage in your presence

I have done Aphrodite's many tasks
Again and again
Until half-blinded and motherless I believe I am without fortitude
This is not the case
My house is still here
My kitchen's full of empty jars for sorting beans and grains
Under the sink are paper cups to rescue spiders

I am vigilant for burns and bites and cuts and scrapes and
breaks and fires and stings
(though I can't see the venom of the wasp)
always listening for my children in the night

When they aren't here sometimes you come
Sharp as an ancient weapon
Winged and dangerous as Eros, listen
My light's meant to reveal and not to burn
I'm done with that I'm done

ORPHEUS

Last night I let myself come
down into the dark
to look for you

(Not you
your memory)

And though I'm almost numb
below the waist
my body woke
to the strokes
of my fingers
remembering your rings
like silver
electricity
igniting me
the quiet wonder in your face
staring between my legs
admiring yourself
avoiding my eyes and mouth
until I took you in
trying to break the barriers
you had so artfully
constructed
over almost a decade
though your spry step
hadn't aged
our conversations
still bright and hopeful
as when we were young
the way you let me circle your hips

with my arms
find your lips
try to break the charm
of her dismissal

Where are you now
to take my hand
and lead me to the bed
the hotel room
with scarf-draped lamps
overlooking jacarandas
fairy lights
the lion in the fountain
the plaza where I last
sat with you and didn't cry
like that couple made of iron?

This whole sweet city
had become a metaphor
for what existed

Now you give me
only written words
reserved
polite
wondering
if I'm all right
but not your voice
your hands
your art
your songs
your length
where I once lay

in harder light of day
no makeup and my hair
a mess
remembering the night
vanilla candlelight
and music
reverb in our organs

Tell me, Eurydice
Boy, where have you been?
What have you learned in hell?
(She found another and did not
come back; you love her still?)

I have learned this

I don't possess such magic to
bring you
or him
or her
or anyone
back
from anywhere
(or hell)

EURYDICE

Remember when we lay together drinking wine from the
amphora and you played your lyre and sang to me?
Our lips were stained and then my breasts
The cypress trees swayed ever so
slightly and even the birds stopped singing to listen
when I was stung by that serpent of our grief and carried way
                                            beneath the earth

where no thing blooms
You came to find me, but I was already Hades' girl
You could charm the trees, the birds, the boatman and all
those walking dead but it was not enough
Even your song could not save me
Only my own will ever bring me back to life
And if those maenads of lust dismember you and you
                                              become a tree
I will lie at your roots and feed you with my blood
And in this way again will we be one

HARPIES

Yesterday at the Roman villa
I saw a lot of things you'd really like
Aphrodite's torso
made of tears and sunlight
glittering in its case
and the heavy gold necklace with the flower
that I imagined pulsing at my collarbone
like a nymph imprisoned in amethyst
and the pointed-toed, red leather shoes with golden trim
belonging to a long-dead girl
buried with her bangles and her toys
making her seem like someone
not just dust

But best of all was Orpheus
his hands stretched out before him
holding a long-gone lyre
flanked by taloned harpies
a reminder
that, in spite of beauty
death is inevitable
and Eurydice
could not be saved

Let's break in at night
drink wine from a kylix
bathe in a shell-paved fountain
filled with water lilies

You would wear the metal helmets
with the slits for eyes

I would wear rock crystal
and the dead girl's shoes

We'd fuck in a sarcophagus
dance for lyre-less Orpheus
while those voiceless harpies sing

CIRCE AND ULYSSES

I've been waiting for you on this island far too long
You are bigger, stronger than any of the others
You hurt but good, the way I've always longed it
You taste of sea and ache there to return
empty yourself into that vastness where everything is born

I want to tell my history
can you hear my words?
how I've been unsatisfied
It makes a woman witchly

When I found myself alone
I built my house with magics
when I found myself thrice-scorned
I men to beasts transformed
padding round my door

Oh Ulysses, here I was
awaiting your arrival
I've been so sad, so mute
so wet and lonely for so long

Ulysses, I don't want
to hold you here forever
against your own desires

Just remember this
with you here inside me
I no longer yearn
to turn men into swine

PSYCHE AND PAN

Psyche realized that maybe she was wrong
maybe Cupid would never appear to her again
She remembered their conversation differently now
"I've moved on," he'd said
There was no mistaking it

Psyche was tired of tasks
her heart hung on by threads of blood
so she called Pan

Fearing danger
she got on anyway
The bike thrummed between her thighs
She shut her eyes
and clung
to Pan's fierce body
as they rode into the night

He'd told her that a woman's sex
could also conjure death
which is why men were so afraid

Was Pan afraid?
Or was he brave
With his sharp hooves and legs of fur

Perhaps, she thought
as they growled along the road
into the music-dark:
he simply had a death wish
and she had one, too

TO HADES

If you give me pomegranate seeds
I'll stay with you below the ground
in clubs aflood with piss and beer
where boys wear horns and sing
so hard they bleed my ears

But now my mother's gone from me
I'm not escaping but her heir
as much winter as the spring
I must return above it seems
They only last so long these things

I've little ones to tend to there
feed and keep them warm
I have a world of light above
I have a willow-thatched home
and little ones to love

The question is, my captor fair
Hades with your grin
your knife-strong core, your mirror
your wild lips and your fingertips
will you join me here?

PART III: FABLES

THE SANDMAN

I made him of black sand
still wet from the ocean
his lips were plums
his legs were small trees
his hands were palm fronds
his sex an obelisk
his ribs were the cage of an ibis

I laid my head on his chest and some grains
got into my eyes
and I dreamed
of how the Sandman
came to life
slid himself inside me
and obliterated my fears for just one night

Oh, Sandman return with your dreams
but in exchange
you may not have my eyes
to feed your children
in their nest on the moon
made of iron

DEATH

Death numbs and disorganizes
but the C word is a motherfucker
no matter how you slice it

Death can be kind, a poet
with long white fingers
He says, "I must take her to the parlor"
He is polite
While the other eats blood in gobs, mouthfuls of tissue
disintegrates and erodes, sucks and belches, burps and laughs
with a mouth like a fat fish

Death took my mother for a walk in his garden
She wore pink pajamas and held his arm
There were lanterns made of rice paper
The trees were hung with cowbells
Somewhere, a voice was singing

Cancer lay curled in my mother's belly
Trying to make her his puppet
She refused
bargained cordially with Death
who bowed his head and nodded
then walked off whistling softly
the winner
with a petal in his tailcoat pocket

PROGENY OF EVILS

The Queen knows these things
She has had long days and nights indistinguishable
under the earth brooding about the state of the world above
Once she stood in a meadow and wept because of fire and flood
disease and death
still she had no idea how prophetic were her words
That strange illness that poured itself between bodies
through the elixir of the blood
wasting men before their time
their faces sunken and lumped from the drugs
no immune systems to speak of and all because they loved
The Queen's own husband had his share of male paramours
It angered her enough to change the seasons
But she had sense
not to destroy the world
She cowered in her lair
maybe it was better here
She no longer missed the world
It was only her daughter
she needed

TAM LIN

The Queen had made me into something
less than human
and already plucked
one of my eyes

I rode half-blind
through wintered rain
The man stepped out into my path
and fell I from my steed
into his arms

"Beware," I said
but he, he only laughed
as I turned into first a bird
then feral cat
then corybantic dog

He held me, still

And when I'd regained
human form
naked as the day was born
with double rose upon my breasts
I held him back

THE DEVIL

The devil wears a Persian cat upon his head
He has a house with endless rooms
fun house mirrors on each wall
so everyone appears
stretched and warped as he
The bombs exploding in the distance
are music to his ears

The devil eats polar bear meat
watches news clippings about global warming and the KKK
and laughs in a high strange way
"It's all made up!"

He is very self-satisfied this beast
He masturbates to images in gossip rags
while his toenails are pared and buffed
By the light of his World War II lamp shade
that looks disturbingly like human skin

But above all
when the devil goes to sleep at night
in his downy emu feather bed
he sighs
closes his eyes
and dreams in peace
for he believes he is not the god of hell
but only a great showman
a great artiste

FREAK SHOW

What's it to you, Mister?
Starin' at me like that
like I'm some kind of frickin' freak

Who gives a rat
that I wear my heart
hangin' right round my neck
a big bloody trophy?
That my skin is scarred with all them
self-made wounds?
I'm a self-made thing!
with my tale writ large

Do you really give a fuck that my back sprouts wings
out of the cartilage—thin fierce whirs?

What's it to you, old man?

I'm fish scales and goat hooves and claw feet and cat tails
I'm teeth and I'm flesh and I'm hair in the places
you didn't approve
I'm your greatest nightmare and the thing you want to own
a sideshow in a cage
a trophy on your wall

In another time and place they'd give me a different name
my friend
they'd call me artist
they'd call me woman
they'd call me god

ABOUT THE AUTHOR

FRANCESCA LIA BLOCK (www.francescaliablock.com) has written more than twenty-five books including *Dangerous Angels: The Weetzie Bat Books*, *The Elementals* and *Beyond the Pale Motel*. She received the Spectrum Award, the Phoenix Award, the ALA Rainbow Award, the 2005 Margaret A. Edwards Lifetime Achievement Award, and other citations from the American Library Association and from the *New York Times Book Review, School Library Journal* and *Publisher's Weekly*. Her work has been translated into Italian, French, German Japanese, Danish, Norwegian, Swedish, Finnish and Portuguese. Francesca teaches fiction workshops at UCLA Extension, Antioch University and privately in Los Angeles.

A Midsummer Night's Press: was founded by Lawrence Schimel in New Haven, CT in 1991. Using a letterpress, it published broadsides of poems by Nancy Willard, Joe Haldeman, and Jane Yolen, among others, in signed, limited editions of 126 copies, numbered 1-100 and lettered A-Z. It now publishes commercially printed titles primarily under the imprints:

Fabula Rasa: devoted to works inspired by mythology, folklore, and fairy tales. Titles from this imprint include *Fairy Tales for Writers* by Lawrence Schimel, *Fortune's Lover: A Book of Tarot Poems* by Rachel Pollack, *Fairy Tales in Electri-city* by Francesca Lia Block, *The Last Selchie Child* by Jane Yolen, *What If What's Imagined Were All True* by Roz Kaveney, and *Lilith's Demons* by Julie R. Enszer.

Body Language: devoted to texts exploring questions of gender and sexual identity. Titles from this imprint include *This is What Happened in Our Other Life* by Achy Obejas; *Banalities* by Brane Mozetic, translated from the Slovene by Elizabeta Zargi with Timothy Liu; *Handmade Love* by Julie R. Enszer; *Mute* by Raymond Luczak; *Milk and Honey: A Celebration of Jewish Lesbian Poetry* edited by Julie R. Enszer; *Dialectic of the Flesh* by Roz Kaveney; *Fortunate Light* by David Bergman; *Deleted Names* by Lawrence Schimel, *This Life Now* by Michael Broder; *When I Was Straight* by Julie Marie Wade; and *Our Lady of the Crossword* by Rigoberto González.

Periscope: devoted to works of poetry in translation by women writers. The first tiles are: *One is None* by Estonian poet Kätlin Kaldmaa (translated by Miriam McIlfatrick), *Anything Could Happen* by Slovenian poet Jana Putrle Srdic (translated by Barbara Jursa), *Dissection* by Spanish poet Care Santos (translated by Lawrence Schimel), and *Caravan Lullabies* by Ilzė Butkutė (translated by Rimas Uzgiris).

www.ingramcontent.com/pod-product-compliance
Lightning Source LLC
Chambersburg PA
CBHW030132100526
44591CB00009B/618